Ocean Animals

Written by Josephine Selwyn

Picture Dictionary

dolphin

fish

octopus

Read the picture dictionary. You will find these words in the book.

shark

turtle

whale

This is a fish.
It lives in the ocean.

fin

This is a shark.
It lives in the ocean.

teeth

This is a turtle.
It lives in the ocean.

shell

This is a dolphin.
It lives in the ocean.

flippers

This is a whale.
It lives in the ocean.

tail

This is an octopus.
It lives in the ocean.

tentacle

Activity Page

1. Draw a turtle.

2. Label these parts:
   shell   legs   head   neck
   eyes   mouth

Do you know
the dictionary words?